TABLE OF CONTENTS

CHAPTER 1

Is Life out There?

Are we alone in the universe? People throughout history have wondered if life exists beyond Earth. Many scientists work to find out the answer. Come along as we search for life in the universe!

The Milky Way Galaxy as seen from Earth

ARE WE ALONE?

Searching for Life Beyond Earth with The Planetary Society®

BRUCE BETTS, PhD

Lerner Publications ◆ Minneapolis

The universe is huge and full of amazing planets, stars, and other worlds. We have not explored many of these worlds, so could life be found somewhere other than Earth? Scientists are working to find the answer.

The Planetary Society® empowers people around the world to advance space science and exploration. On behalf of The Planetary Society®, including our tens of thousands of members, here's to wishing you the joy of discovery.

Onward,

Bill Nye

Bill Nye
CEO, The Planetary Society®

ALIEN LIFE

What do you picture when you think of life on other planets? Maybe you picture the aliens you see on TV or in movies. But we don't know if alien life exists or what it would look like. We also don't know if it would be intelligent.

People have created models and art of what they think alien life could look like.

Most scientists agree that there is no evidence of life beyond Earth or of alien life visiting Earth. So why do we think it might be out there?

Space is huge and filled with many planets and other worlds. At least one hundred billion stars are in the Milky Way Galaxy. And our universe has at least one hundred billion galaxies. That means we haven't explored a lot of worlds where alien life could be found.

Artwork of the Milky Way Galaxy

The large telescope Gemini North studies stars.

It is hard to study distant stars because they are so far away from Earth. And it is hard to send spacecraft to the other planets in our solar system.

But scientists are looking for life. They use spacecraft in our solar system and telescopes to look beyond it. They also work to understand why there is life on Earth.

SPACECRAFT STUDIES

Different types of spacecraft are used to study other worlds. Some see if life is possible there. One example is the Perseverance rover. It explores Mars.

CHAPTER 2

Life on Earth

Understanding life on Earth helps scientists know how and where to look for life on other worlds. You find life everywhere you go on Earth. Life includes plants, people, and other animals.

Life also includes microbes such as bacteria. Microbes are very tiny. You need to use a microscope to see them.

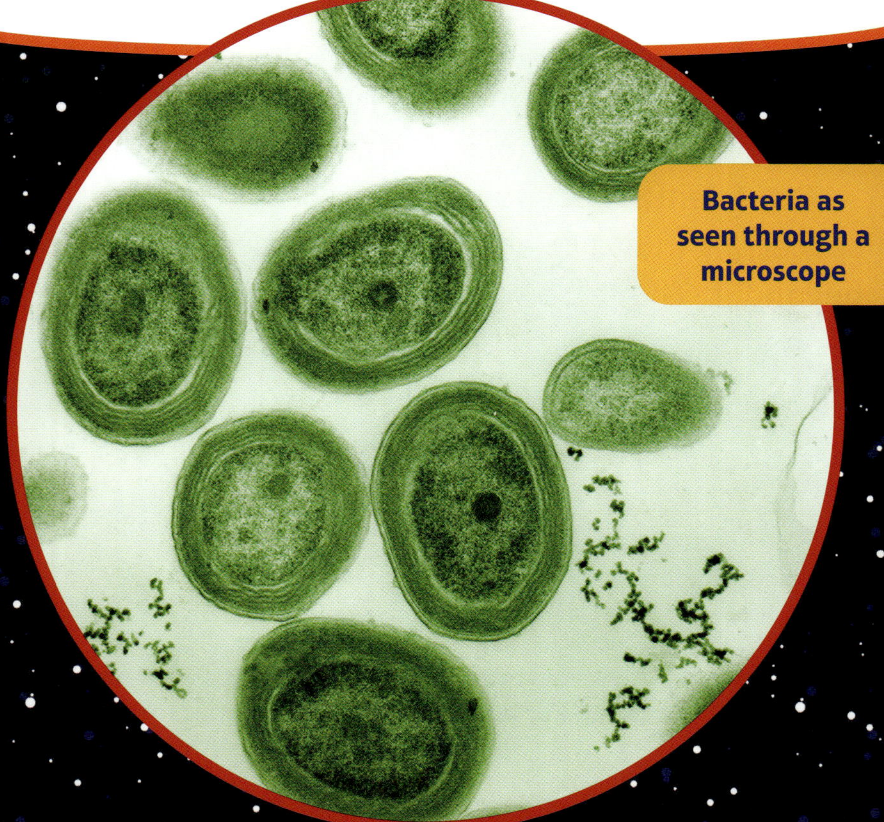

Bacteria as seen through a microscope

Earth as seen from space

Earth is about 4.5 billion years old. Fossils show evidence of life from very early on in that history.

Fossils can be billions of years old.

THINGS ALL LIFE NEEDS

How do we know where to look for life besides Earth? We look at places that have the three things all life on Earth needs.

The first thing is liquid water. Water can be ice, a gas, or a liquid.

Life and liquid water on Earth

Animals and plants are made mostly of the same six elements.

The second thing is a small number of elements. These are called the building blocks of life. They combine to form almost everything in your body and make up almost all living things on Earth.

BUILDING BLOCKS OF LIFE

There are six elements that life needs. They are carbon, hydrogen, nitrogen, oxygen, phosphorus, and sulfur.

Life around hot water coming up from the ocean floor

The third thing is energy. Most life gets energy from sunlight. Plants use sunlight as energy to live and grow. Humans get energy from eating plants or the animals that ate the plants.

Some places on the ocean floor have life that does not need sunlight. This life gets energy from the chemicals in hot water coming up from cracks in the ocean floor.

LIFE IN MANY PLACES

Some microbes and other Earth life can live in harsh places. Some live in very hot water. Others live in areas where it is below freezing. That means life might also be found in more harsh places in the universe.

The Grand Prismatic Spring in Yellowstone National Park is home to lots of bacteria.

CHAPTER 3

Searching for Solar System Life

The solar system is everything that goes around the Sun. This includes planets and moons. All the objects in our solar system are very far from one another. That makes it hard to study them and search for life.

Is there life or has there ever been life elsewhere in the solar system? Any life is likely tiny and simple. You would need a microscope to see it.

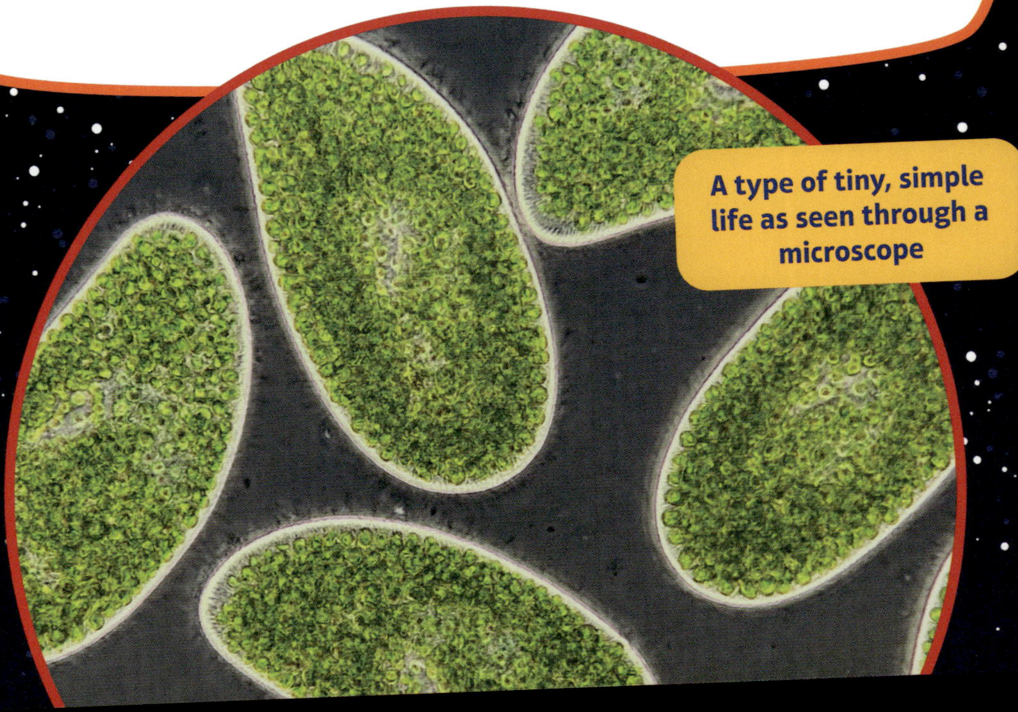

A type of tiny, simple life as seen through a microscope

The NASA Curiosity rover explores Mars.

HOW AND WHERE TO LOOK

Scientists use telescopes to study the planets and other worlds that are far from Earth. But spacecraft can give us a closer view. Some spacecraft fly by or go into orbit around those worlds. Other spacecraft such as landers and rovers explore the surface of the worlds.

There are many worlds to explore. But spacecraft are expensive. It also takes years for them to get to the other worlds. Scientists must choose carefully where to explore.

Art showing the Europa Clipper arriving at Jupiter's moon Europa in 2030

What do scientists look for when searching worlds for life? The first thing is liquid water.

Earth is the only place in our solar system that has liquid water on its surface. But some worlds may have had liquid water in the past. And some may have liquid water below their surface.

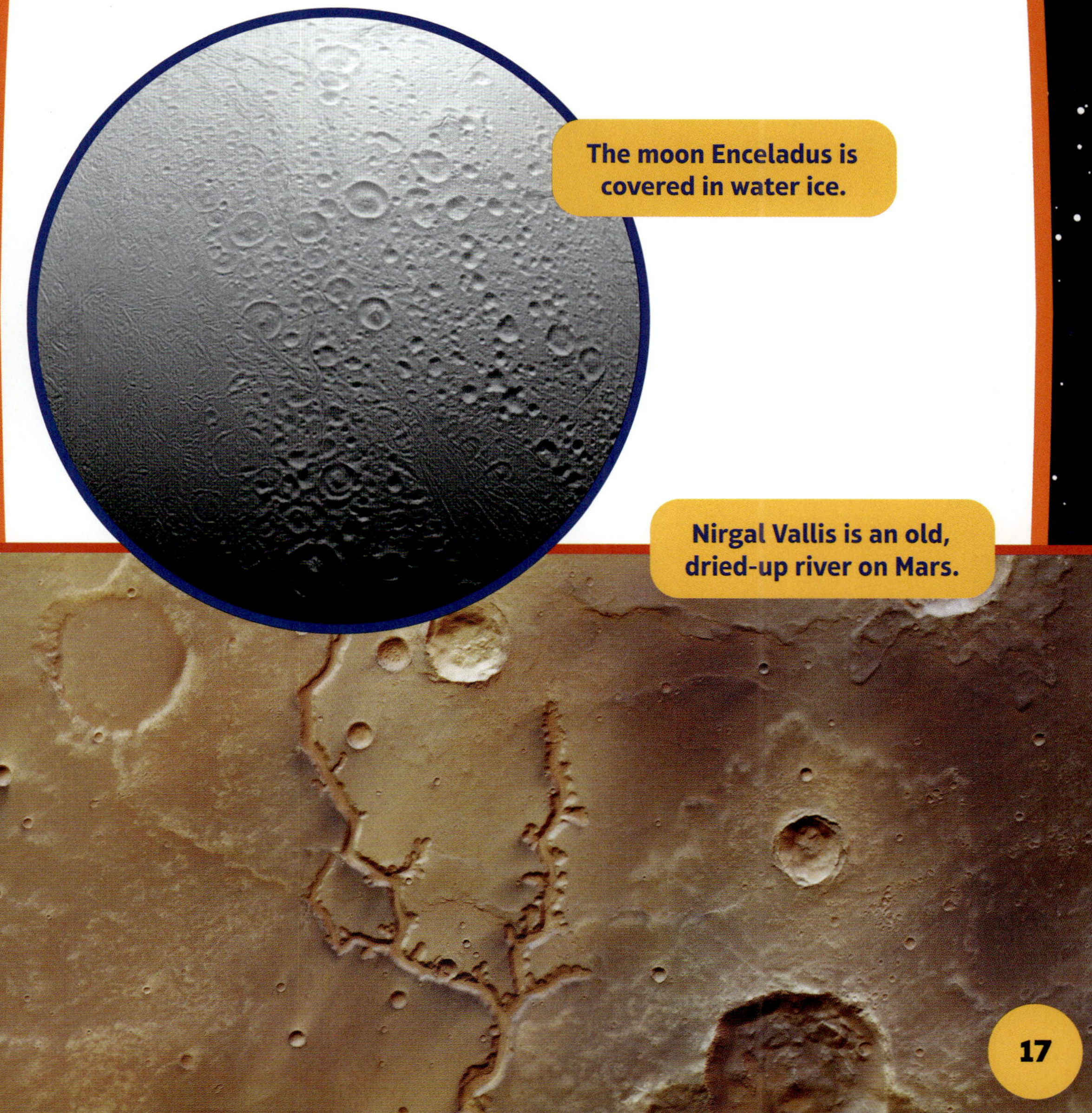

The moon Enceladus is covered in water ice.

Nirgal Vallis is an old, dried-up river on Mars.

MARS

The surface of Mars is unlikely to support life. Mars is very cold and has little atmosphere. It has almost no oxygen, which we need to breathe.

Mars may have very small amounts of liquid water on the surface for a few minutes or hours at a time. But the cold temperature and thin atmosphere almost always make water on Mars a gas or ice.

An image of Mars taken by spacecraft

Mars had a lot of liquid water and a thicker atmosphere in the past. Spacecraft pictures show rocks that were cut by old rivers and giant floods a long time ago.

Rovers have studied rocks from the surface. They have found that liquid water used to flow. There are plans to take some Mars rocks to Earth to look for evidence of past life.

Teardrop-shaped islands on Mars that were formed by huge floods

Europa close up

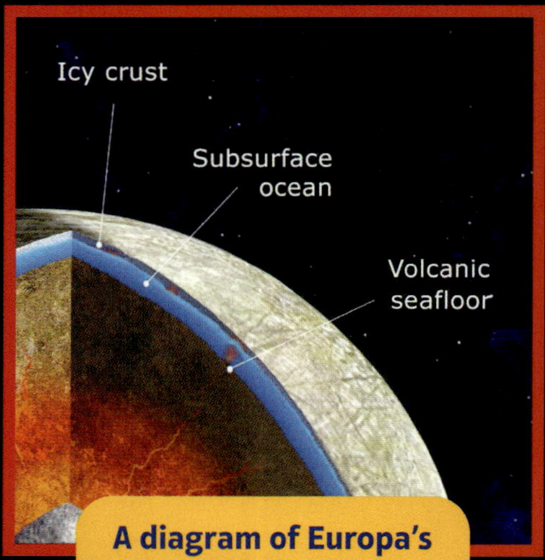

A diagram of Europa's possible interior

ICE WORLDS

Europa is one of Jupiter's moons. Its surface is made of cracked water ice. A liquid water ocean is below miles of ice.

No sunlight reaches the ocean, which has a rocky bottom. It may have cracks like in Earth's ocean where chemicals in hot water can come out. That means Europa could also have life in its ocean.

SIZE OF EUROPA

Europa is smaller than Earth and the Moon. But Europa's ocean has about twice as much liquid water as Earth's oceans.

Saturn's moon Enceladus is also covered in water ice. Scientists think it has a liquid water ocean under miles of ice. Rock pieces in the ice show the ocean likely has a rocky bottom.

One part of the ice surface has deep cracks. The Cassini spacecraft sampled sprays of water ice from these cracks. The water freezes when it erupts into space.

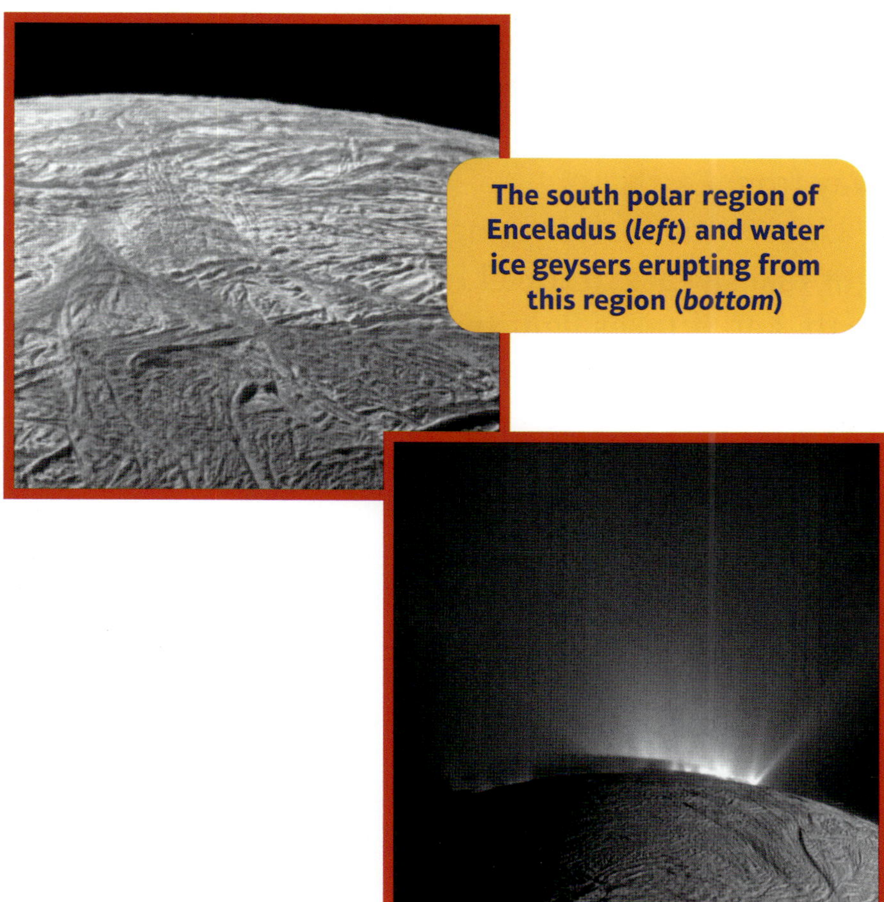

The south polar region of Enceladus (*left*) and water ice geysers erupting from this region (*bottom*)

CHAPTER 4

Looking Beyond Our Solar System

It is not easy to look for life beyond our solar system. Everything outside of our solar system is super far away from Earth.

Light is the fastest thing in the universe. But even light takes years to travel from the closest stars to Earth. And it takes light two million years to reach us from the Andromeda Galaxy.

The Andromeda Galaxy is one of the closest galaxies to us.

EXOPLANETS

An exoplanet is a planet around another star. The first was discovered in 1992. We have found thousands more since then.

We can't send spacecraft to exoplanets because they are too far from Earth. Even big telescopes often can't see them. The star is usually too bright for us to see the much dimmer exoplanet.

One way astronomers find an exoplanet is by seeing changes in a star's brightness. The star appears to dim if an exoplanet passes in front of it. That shows that an exoplanet is there.

Art of an exoplanet passing in front of its star

Art that imagines what Kepler-186f might look like

Scientists use what we know of life on Earth to look for exoplanets that might support life. The exoplanet would likely be about the size of Earth. It would also likely be rocky with a solid surface.

KEPLER-186F

Kepler-186f is an exoplanet that is about the size of Earth. Scientists discovered it in 2014 using the Kepler space telescope.

Scientists also look at the habitable zone of an exoplanet's star. That area is sometimes called the Goldilocks zone. It is the distance from the star where liquid water could exist on the surface of an exoplanet.

The zone's temperature is not too hot and not too cold. It is just right.

A diagram of the habitable zone

Newer telescopes such as the James Webb Space Telescope can sometimes look at what exoplanet atmospheres are made of. Certain gases in an atmosphere could hint at life.

Earth's atmosphere has a lot of oxygen. There is so much oxygen because plants have created most of it. An exoplanet with a lot of oxygen may have life.

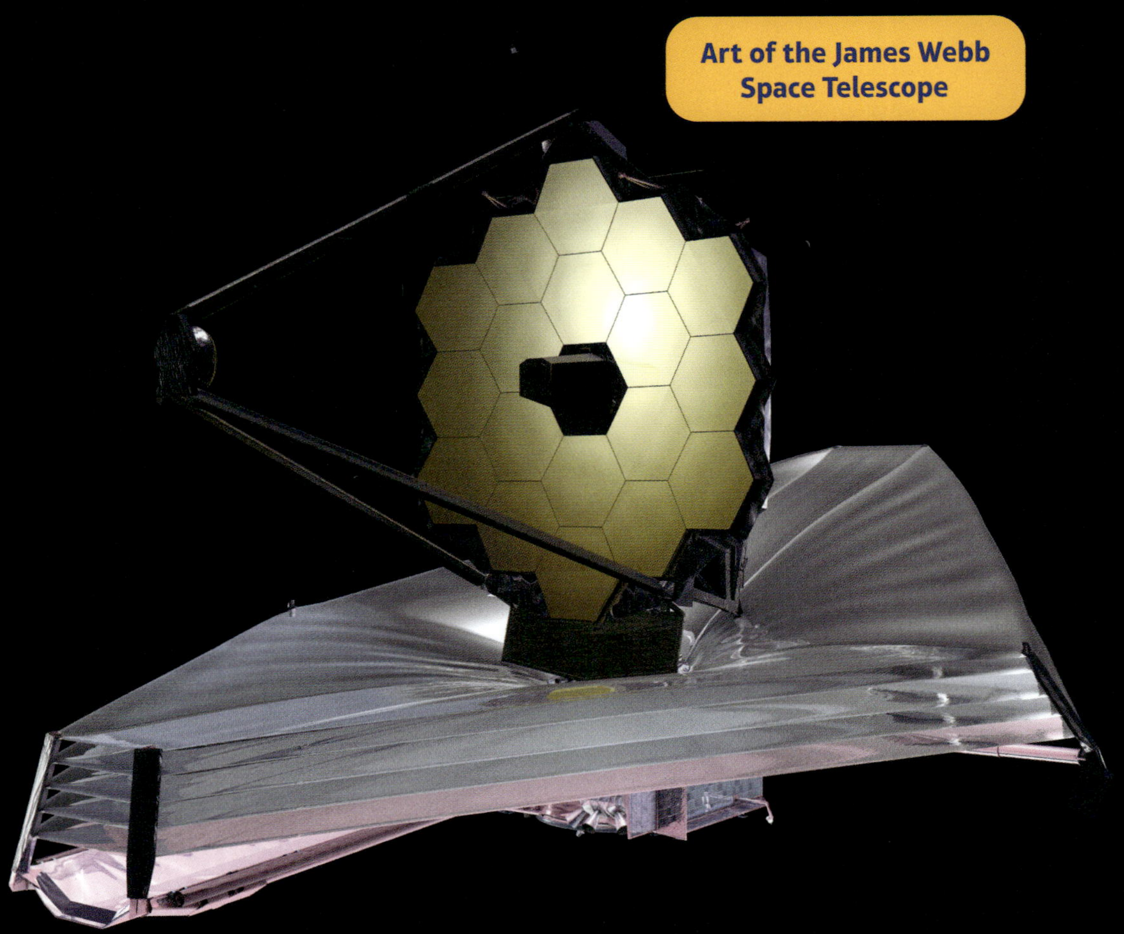

Art of the James Webb Space Telescope

ALIEN SIGNALS

Some scientists look for signals from distant life. These would be messages from intelligent aliens.

Many searches have used large radio dishes to listen for alien signals. Some searches have used special telescopes to look for laser flashes. Current searches often look at the most Earthlike exoplanets that have been found.

The Green Bank Telescope in West Virginia

Scientists have not found any messages from aliens. But we've only looked at a little bit of the huge universe. We also don't know when, from where, or how aliens would send signals.

The Planetary Society Optical SETI Telescope at Harvard searched the sky for laser signals.

We have not found life beyond Earth. Is it out there? We don't know. But our tech and understanding of Earth life keep getting better.

Finding life beyond Earth could be the biggest discovery in history! We would finally know that we are not alone.

Galaxies as seen by the James Webb Space Telescope

GLOSSARY

atmosphere: the gases surrounding a planet, moon, or other body

chemical: a substance that has a specific makeup

element: a substance made of one thing that can't be broken down into anything simpler

evidence: information that can be used to prove something is true or false

exoplanet: a planet that orbits a star that is not the Sun

galaxy: a collection of millions, billions, or even trillions of stars as well as dust and gas all held together in one group by gravity. We live in the Milky Way Galaxy.

intelligent: having a great ability to learn, think, and understand

microbe: also known as a microorganism, a living thing small enough that it can only be seen with a microscope

orbit: the path a planet, moon, or other object follows as it goes around another object

planet: a big, round, ball-shaped object that only goes around the Sun. Our solar system has eight planets. A planet does not have anything close to the same size near its orbit.

spacecraft: a vehicle or object made for travel in outer space

LEARN MORE

Betts, Bruce, PhD. *Mars: The Red Planet*. Minneapolis: Lerner Publications, 2025.

Britannica Kids: Extraterrestrial Life
https://kids.britannica.com/students/article/extraterrestrial-life/274243

ESA Kids: What Is an Exoplanet?
https://www.esa.int/kids/en/learn/Lessons/What_is_an_exoplanet

Mazzarella, Kerri. *Jupiter.* Coral Springs, FL: Seahorse, 2023.

NASA Space Place
https://spaceplace.nasa.gov

The Planetary Society: The Best Places to Search for Life in Our Solar System
https://www.planetary.org/articles/the-best-places-to-search-for-life-in-our-solar-system

INDEX

PHOTO ACKNOWLEDGMENTS

Image credits: F. Scott Schafer/The Planetary Society, p. 2; ESO/B. Tafreshi (twanight.org), p. 4; NASA/Bill Ingalls, p. 5; NASA/JPL-Caltech/R. Hurt (SSC/Caltech), p. 6; International Gemini Observatory/NOIRLab/NSF/AURA/J. Pollard, p. 7; Luke Thompson from Chisholm Lab and Nikki Watson from Whitehead, MIT/Wikimedia Commons (PD), p. 8; NASA Goddard Space Flight Center Image by Reto Stöckli/Robert Simmon/MODIS, p. 9 (top); GeoStock/Getty Images, p. 9 (bottom); Bruce Betts, pp. 10–11; Courtesy of the NOAA Ocean Exploration, 2016 Deepwater Exploration of the Marianas, p. 12; Ronnie Wiggin/Getty Images, p. 13; Daniel J. Wieczynski/Duke University/National Science Foundation, p. 14; NASA/JPL-Caltech/MSSS/Anadolu/Getty Images, p. 15; NASA/JPL-Caltech, p. 16; NASA/JPL-Caltech/Space Science Institute, pp. 17 (top), 21 (bottom); ESA/DLR/FU Berlin, p. 17 (bottom); NASA/JPL/Malin Space Science Systems, p. 18; NASA/JPL-Caltech/ASU, p. 19; NASA/JPL-Caltech/SETI Institute, p. 20 (left); NASA/JPL-Caltech/Michael Carroll, p. 20 (right); NASA/JPL/Space Science Institute, p. 21 (top); Torben Hansen/Wikimedia Commons (CC), p. 22; ESO/L. Calçada, p. 23; NASA/Ames/JPL-Caltech/T. Pyl, p. 24; NASA/Petigura/UC Berkeley, Howard/UH-Manoa, Marcy/UC Berkeley, p. 25; NASA, p. 26; NRAO/AUI/National Science Foundation, p. 27; The Planetary Society, p. 28; NASA/ESA/CSA/STScI, p. 29. Design elements: A Mokhtari/Getty Images; bamlou/Getty Images.

Cover: NASA/ESA/CSA/STScI; NASA/ESA/CSA/STScI/Janice Lee (STScI), Thomas Williams (Oxford)/Rupali Chandar (UToledo)/Daniela Calzetti (UMass)/PHANGS Team.

FOR MY SONS, DANIEL AND KEVIN, AND FOR ALL THE MEMBERS OF THE PLANETARY SOCIETY®

Lerner Publications Company
An imprint of Lerner Publishing Group, Inc.
241 First Avenue North
Minneapolis, MN 55401 USA

For reading levels and more information, look up this title at www.lernerbooks.com.

Main body text set in Aptifer Sans LT Pro.
Typeface provided by Linotype AG.

Editor: Brianna Kaiser **Designer:** Mary Ross **Photo Editor:** Angel Kidd

Library of Congress Cataloging-in-Publication Data

Names: Betts, Bruce, PhD, author. | The Planetary Society.
Title: Are we alone? : searching for life beyond Earth with The Planetary Society / Bruce Betts, PhD.
Description: Minneapolis, MN : Lerner Publications, [2026] | Includes bibliographical references and index. | Audience: Ages 7–10 | Audience: Grades 2–3 | Summary: "The universe is massive, so is it possible that there is life beyond Earth? Readers will discover the ins and outs of life in outer space and the technology and research being used to find answers"— Provided by publisher.
Identifiers: LCCN 2024046219 (print) | LCCN 2024046220 (ebook) | ISBN 9798765668221 (library binding) | ISBN 9798765684672 (paperback) | ISBN 9798765680131 (epub)
Subjects: LCSH: Life on other planets—Juvenile literature.
Classification: LCC QB54 .B47 2026 (print) | LCC QB54 (ebook) | DDC 576.8/39—dc23/eng/20250102

LC record available at https://lccn.loc.gov/2024046219
LC ebook record available at https://lccn.loc.gov/2024046220

Manufactured in the United States of America
1-1011914-53790-2/13/2025